NOT EASY BEING ME

Copyright © 2020 by ANITA 'NIKKI' GIBBS

Unless otherwise noted, Scripture quotations are from the NIV Study Bible & New King James Version Copyright © 1982 by Thomas Nelson, Inc. Used by permission. Quotations identified as NIV are from The Holy Bible, New International Version®, NIV® Copyright ©1973, 1978, 1984, 2011 by Biblica, Inc.® Used by permission. All rights reserved worldwide. Quotation identified HCSB are from the Holman Christian Standard Bible®, Copyright © 1999, 2000, 2002, 2003, 2009 by Holman Bible Publishers. Quotations identified as NLT are from The *Holy Bible,* New Living Translation, copyright ©1996, 2004, 2007. Used by permission of Tyndale House Publishers, Inc., Carol Stream, Illinois 60188. All Rights Reserved. Quotations identified as BSB are from the Berean Study Bible (BSB) © 2016 by Bible Hub and Berean Bible

Used by Permission. All rights Reserved. Quotations identified as KJV are from the Holman KJV Study Bible Copyright ©2012 By Holman Bible Publishers Nashville, Tennessee. All Rights Reserved Quotations identified as KJV are from Bible Study Notes, King's English Glossary, and KJV Bible Concordance Copyright © 2012 by Holman Bible Publishers Nashville, Tennessee. All Rights Reserved. Quotation labeled Aramaic Bible in Plain English is from the Original Aramaic New Testament in Plain English-with Psalms & Proverbs Copyright © 2007; 8th edition Copyright © 2013 All rights reserved. Used by Permission

The examples and characters presented in this book are based on the author's actual life events throughout the years. The orientation, identities and names have been changed to protect the innocent. Any resemblance is coincidental.

ISBN - 978-0-578-73272-5

NOT EASY BEING ME
MEMOIR OF A FEMALE ARMY VETERAN

ANITA 'NIKKI' GIBBS

TABLE OF CONTENTS

DEDICATION: .... **IX**

CHAPTER 1: Decisions 1
CHAPTER 2: One Wish 6
CHAPTER 3: The Hallways of Hell 9
CHAPTER 4: College Days 12
CHAPTER 5: Don't Ask, Don't Tell 16
CHAPTER 6: Here's the Thing 25
CHAPTER 7: Bumps in The Road 30
CHAPTER 8: The Finest City 40
CHAPTER 9: The Agony of The Sanctuary 50
CHAPTER 10: The Missing Piece 56
POETRY:
    AT LAST 62
    FIRST SIGHT 63
    THE LAST TIME 64
    BROKEN 65
    ONCE LOVED 66
CHAPTER 11: Good Grief 67
FINAL NOTE: 69

DEDICATION

This book is dedicated to my mother, Deborah Ann T. Gibbs, who taught me responsibility, strength, and to have faith in God, at a young age. To my family who have always allowed me to be myself, no matter what. I have tried to make sure that you all knew how valuable you are to me. Also, to the memory of my beloved uncle, Kenneth E. Thompson, who taught me many life lessons from the Bible. Every year, while sitting around the Thanksgiving table, he would mention God and his plans to travel the world after retirement. I will never forget those moments we shared.

Also, the loving memory of my grandmother, Eva Pearl Christina T. Kirkpatrick. She taught me honesty, courage and always to tell it like it is. I hope that I have made her proud.

Give Honor Where Honor Is Due

Do not withhold good from those to whom it is due, when it is in your power to act.

Proverbs 3:27

CHAPTER ONE
Decisions

SECURITY! SECURITY!

"Alright, if you don't stop in five, four, three, two... okay. Now, where were we? I told you what would happen to you if you tried me!" I could not breathe and was grasping for air. This three-hundred-pound man was smothering me. I couldn't push him off me, no matter how hard I tried. My body would not move. Tears and snot ran down my face. There was a filthy rag in my mouth and my hands were tied to a pole. I was covered in his nasty semen and sweat. What happened to my legs? I couldn't feel my legs! They were numb.

"Get up! Amanda! Get off the floor now! "I need you back in the chair."

"Huh?", I replied. "What just happened here? I told you, hypnosis couldn't work on me."

"Tell me about your pain Sergeant Bobbit."

"I can't explain it, Dr. Stephens."

"C'mon, we have forty-five minutes to give it a try."

"Sir, which pain do you speak of? Is it the physical, mental, emotional, spiritual, or psychological pain?"

"I want to know everything about Amanda Gilbert-Bobbit." Dr. H. Stephens stated. "I want to start at the beginning, Mrs. Gilbert."

"There are many types of pain when it comes to me, Dr. Stephens. I have the physical pain, which includes migraines and headaches."

The Accident

I fell from the top of a five-ton truck while stationed in Fort Bragg. I hit my head on the pavement and I was knocked unconscious. I have no idea how long I was down. I was awakened and picked up by soldiers.

My only thought was, I would be taken to the TMC, Troop Medical Center. Boy! I was completely shocked when they took me to the field instead. The platoon leader told me, "You'll be alright with all that behind!"

"Let's move it, Soldier!" Later that night, I was rushed to the TMC for headaches. I have had them every day since February 1997. Sometimes the migraines last five hours. The sunlight, loud music, loud voices on the phone, and unusual senses aggravated them. My lumbar sprain, sciatica, and hip pain kept me up at night. The hip pain that was aggravated when I sleep, sit, drive, and walk was unbearable. The knee injury came from basic training and running over the years. The thigh contusion from an accident while working, came from working at the United Parcel Service (UPS). I also had a torn rotator cuff that limited the amount of weight I could carry.

There were many mornings where I could barely walk. I'd wake up early because I knew how devastating the pain could be and I knew that I needed to get early morning starts. I had to massage my legs, hip, and right arm to get the blood flowing just to function. Some days the pain took hours to go away.

I cried every night for about fifteen years. I asked and begged God to heal me. I would lay on the bed reaching out toward the ceiling and yelling, "Lord please!" I laid there in excruciating pain. It felt like something was ripping my bones in my lower body. My head would be pounding as if I were getting hit with a hammer on the right side. Tears and snot rolled down my face.

Sharp pains streaked down my right legs. It felt as if someone was stabbing me. I wanted to call 911 but, chose not to. I wanted to keep it to myself. Oddly, I felt a sense of embarrassment about my pain.

"Ugh! The ankle, this ankle!" I cried at times. It hurt whenever it wanted to. I dealt with it the best I could. "I cannot let this chronic pain hold me down." I would say to myself, "I have faith in God. He is a healer and by His stripes, I am healed." I would say. I worked hard at encouraging myself.

"Let's chat about your childhood." Dr. Stephens demanded. Of course, I grew up in a very close-knit family. Our mom had always been the provider, protector, and profess how much she cared.

My Dad, I didn't get to know well. He was murdered on my graduation night. He only reached out to me a few times before he died. I spoke with him during the week of my graduation on the phone and he said I would see him at grandmother's house. He wanted pictures of me but died before I could get them to him so, I placed them in the pocket of his suit jacket while he was lying in the casket.

When people say that I am strong, a go-getter, and sharp, I must admit, these traits came from my mom and other women in my family. These ladies had always been my role models. I am proud of them!

"Uhm, are you at peace now Amanda?" "You wouldn't understand Doc! I cannot continue to live in this simple state of mind. No breathing room at times! People getting on my nerves! The users, abusers, and accusers. I don't want to be the next soldier that's found with a bottle in one hand and a gun in the other. One who has suffered from PTSD, TBI, symptoms of MST, migraines, chronic pain, and anxiety. No one cares Dr. Stephens! No one cares at all! I gave this country my youth, strength, honor, dedication, and respect. All I wanted was to be a PROUD AMERICAN who lived freely. What did I get in return? It took me fourteen years to receive benefits! The military doesn't care about me!" I told him.

CHAPTER TWO
One Wish

"I'm off to see the Wizard..." A little song I'd sang on the most dreadful walk home. Seems like the further I walked the darker the path grew. It was my only way home. Only eight years old and attending the elementary school nearby.

The school is around the corner from my house. Oftentimes, I wanted to take the bus to my grandma's house. I waited there until my mom got off work.

The trees had dark eyes, wide mouths, and pointed noses. Why do the branches hang so low? It seemed like they would carry me away. At the end of the path, was a sidewalk that led to my house. Every time I reached it; I began to walk slowly. I would pretend that I was on the *yellow brick road*. I was praying to see the Wizard as my one wish!

First one home again, here he comes! He'd grabbed me by my hair and carried me. My small feet dangled in the air. My mouth covered with one hand and clothes removed with the other. He'd had no care in the world as he took advantage of my innocence. My eyes would be closed, my heart pounded, my mind wandered, and my body was numbed. My one wish was that he would die. I wanted him dead. If not him, just take me, Lord!

Years passed and the memories caused me to hate to ride by my old home. It was on the same street as my church. Sad, but true. I wanted the house to burst into flames. I was so relieved when we moved. I was finally set free from torture, at least for that moment.

I have been afraid to have children of my own. Just the thought of a man doing that to my children bothered me. Those thoughts have tormented me my entire life.

It wasn't until the Spring of 2011, when I began to speak out about my traumas. I started seeing a therapist. I needed help from someone who could assist me with the flashbacks and nightmares involving a monster that visited my dreams. He was tall, dark, with a thick blockhead, and smelled like cigarettes. I hated cigarettes! I'd wake up in cold sweats, breathing heavily and crying. I couldn't believe that a person could be so evil and cruel to a child.

I hated myself for a very long time. I never knew the reason. After careful observation in therapy, I realized that none of the abuse was my fault. Someone should have told that to the villain in my dreams.

Spider-Girl, a vigilante that protected me for so many years. She appeared only in my dreams. She would attack anyone who could cause me physical and mental harm.

She swung from buildings with her web and wore a protective suit. She would turn over cars and trucks. She fought men and boys off. She kept a close eye on events, people and me.

My therapist hated that I created such a person. It was the only time I felt safe. The hardest part was dreaming. Wow! I had to go to sleep to feel safe. Sleep was my friend. Nowadays, I sleep a little more. Spider-Girl has accomplished her mission.

I had finally gotten the nerve to tell my mom about it. That's when I learned that the pedophile had died. I found peace in knowing that the monster was gone! "Thank you Jesus for granting me that wish!"

CHAPTER THREE
The Hallways of Hell

At the age of ten I worked hard to maintain good grades. I had the highest average in most of my classes. It was like I had to make good grades or else. I don't remember being threatened or was I just focused. I am guessing that I had to be focused on something. I was in every play that was featured, on the honor roll, in the school paper, in spelling bees and the most exciting thing of all, on the safety team.

Yep! I was a safety patrol. I had several duties as a patrol. I would protect the students from hazards when crossing roads and highways. I assisted the bus drivers in transporting the students. I often taught the students traffic safety and monitor the hallways. I was responsible and was supposed to be respected.

My greatest task was monitoring the hallways. The students, or should I say, black guys and a few girls would bully me. They would talk about my clothes, shoes, hair, call me jet black, black jap, Ethiopian, Skinny Minnie, and Penny with a hole in it. Although I was very smart and active in school, they would constantly disrespect me and yell at me. I yelled back but, sometimes I'd get spit balls and trash thrown from different directions not knowing from whom. No one would tell.

I guess my little power intimidated them. That's what my guidance counselor would say. I continued to walk with my head held high. I kept up the high averages and did my performances.

The bullying followed me throughout the years to the other schools. I could not be on the cheering squads or apart of any groups. I was on the honor roll, drama clubs, beta clubs, and ROTC at every school. I was a part of the things that really mattered.

A miracle happened when my mom decided to move to another city because of her job. We lost a few friends and had to start another school, but the joy of not being bullied was joyful. My mom never knew.

I would forever remember kids from certain neighborhoods, Roundtree Circle, Torbit St, Center St and Brooklyn that called me names for no reason. I was just a kid. I didn't bother anyone. I was a safety patrol doing my job.

When I attended Northwestern, my life changed. Everything was so different, and the school was huge of course. I met some very kind people. I fit right in! I started driving right away, got a job and things got to rolling.

I still looked back to the old town for my prom date. Bad idea, this guy stood me up. I was looking good too. I went on stag as if nothing happened. I met up with my new bestie AJ. She was the coolest chic in the Air Force ROTC. We clicked right away. She went stag also. I dare anyone to stand me up these days. It will be trouble for him. I mean trouble!

People often asked me why I gave my culture a hard time. What?! Look at all I have been through with them. From the beginning of time. HAHA! I can't stand no more. Lol!

I graduated a year early since being that I was no longer with my original class. Woo hoo! Class of '91, Trojans!

I learned a lot and dealt with so much just from walking the hallways of the school.

CHAPTER FOUR
College Days

Hip hop! don't stop! Here comes the cutie they called Short Stop! Ha!. Those were the good ole days. My earlier years in college. I met such a festive group of ladies. My Girls Philly, Connecticut, D.C., and New York. Yep! Those were my homies. What a fabulous time we had!

My Girls and I would rent cars, took trips, went to parties, saw movies, went to luncheons, took walks, had our own parties, and maintained a great relationship. Usually, a group of our size would more than likely encounter a lot of drama. Not this group of ladies! It was Lopez, Hill, Turpin, Furman and Brown. We all kept in touch. We were family.

My instructor, Sergeant Carroll hooked me up with the babysitting gig. She, Justin and Dominique became my family.
I had so much fun with them. Sergeant Carroll kept in touch with me and my family. She visited me when I had surgery. I'm so glad that I met her.

Although my college days were fun, unlike most students, I had to hold down two jobs and attend classes. I was working at

McDonald's and babysitting part-time. Now that was hard work indeed!

Yes, I still maintained good grades.

I was a member of the ROTC there. (The Reserve Officers Training Course). This course would allow me to enter the Armed Forces as an officer. I was in good shape. I went from slim, trim, skin, and bones to thick and firm. We would do physical training most mornings before class.

I was sent away for eight weeks of training to Ft Knox, Kentucky. It was like a huge camp. Well, that is what they wanted us to believe. It was a form of basic training for officers. Omg! There I experienced the gas chamber, road matches, firing ranges, grenade ranges, land navigation, sleeping in foxholes, etc.

Once I graduated from the camp, I returned to school. I had good grades but could no longer attend classes. I later learned about the college I was attending was embezzling money. Someone in the accounting office had wronged me. Unfortunately, because of the negligence of Benedict, I had to pay the price. So, I made a difficult decision about my life and quit school. Soon after I joined the Armed Forces. I joined the United States Army but, I wasn't commissioned as an officer.

The WU

Fourteen years later I enrolled in another institution, Winthrop University. NOPE! I was not as alert, young, and bright as before. However, I was determined. I was working two jobs again and going full time.

I was a delivery driver full time and part-time at a Boys Home. My job as a delivery driver was very interesting. I was proud to be a clerk as well.

There were not a lot of female drivers in our hub. Often I was harassed by management. I was in a devastating accident, that made the use of my knee difficult. So now I had to deal with harassment, stress, and working while in pain.

I also had to deal with managers' cocky attitudes. Just because someone was in management didn't mean that they were always right. I would be talked down to, trapped in a cage crying with no one to call, and the manager would laugh. I fought hard for my freedom on that job. Thanks to the Union, several managers were replaced, and the hub became a good working environment.

I did my internship at the American Red Cross. I worked with a lot of kindhearted women there. I learned a lot from them as well.

I was able to assist so many people in the community. I taught the girls and boys club fire prevention. I help fire victims with hotels rooms, medical and personal supplies.

I assisted Hurricane Katrina victims that were in the area. I was able to do so much good for others. Doing for others is what Social Work is all about.

I was faced with many challenges while attending the University. I had two major surgeries, was coping with traumatic brain injury (TBI), and the exhaustion of it all. I did not give up though. It was very stressful going to school full time, working full time with craziness, doing an internship, and coping with surgery. I remembered what my elders said, "If you don't stand for something, you'll fall for everything."

I had knee, ankle, and breast surgery and was worried about graduation. Whoo-hoo! I was able to walk across the stage with two shoes on and no crutches.

I was determined to be ready by graduation. I graduated with a BSW degree, Bachelor of Social Work. Never give up, no matter what obstacles you may encounter!

Let us not be weary in doing Good. For we will Reap in due season if we don't give Up.

Galatians 6:9

CHAPTER FIVE
Don't Ask, and Don't Tell
Sweet Jackson

What did 1 do? It is true what folks say, "We do more before nine than some people do all day." Never thought that I would work so much. Physical training, road march, rifle range, classes, and drills in a day. "GI Joe and GI Gravy. I wish I had joined the Navy!" I realized that my life was no longer mine. I had to sleep in foxholes, on the ground in sleeping bags, in a Hemtt truck, on a freaking cot, and in small tents.

It was cold and rainy most days in "Sweet Jackson". I was put in charge. I was the platoon guide (PG). Hmmm!

I didn't know what to expect in this position. I was young and dumb to basic training. I was held responsible for many soldiers. Being the PG was no small cup of tea. I can assure you. One drill sergeant harassed me so badly. He called me Penny and made me get in the push-up position every time he saw me. It wasn't enough to do push-ups, but he'd make me get up, get down, get up and get down until he was tired. That was not funny one bit to me.

Once, I heard a drill sergeant tell a soldier he would throw her out of the window. Now, that made us straighten up quickly. I felt like we were walking on eggshells. We had to tread lightly until we graduated.

I often envied the soldiers that found ways to get out. Although most of the time it was general or dishonorable. I decided to hang in there, no matter what.

Virginia

In AIT, (Advanced Individual Training), I was chosen to be the platoon guide again. The Drill Sergeant said that I seemed to be quiet and shy. It was challenging but fun at first. Little did I know, the title came with a big responsibility. I was there to learn my job and not to be picked on. I was taking the slack for everyone.

Whatever a soldier did or didn't do when asked, I had to take the heat. I advanced from ten push-ups to maxing them out with sixty quickly. It was weird having to do them in my civilian clothes.

No matter what, whenever the drill sergeants saw me coming they made me get down. I didn't appreciate this behavior but, what could I have done? If no one asked, then Wow, who was I going to tell? Often you're told, "Suck it up and move on soldier!"

I would dread the days when I stood in front of the platoon. I knew the harassment was coming. My platoon sergeant would tell me that he wanted me, or he'd say, "I smell you *down there*." or "You look good" or something sexual. I'd be so uncomfortable. No one heard him because I stood a distance from the others. I'd just listen as I stood at parade rest. What are soldiers supposed to do when they are put in that type of situation?

Texas

Ole Fort Hood was up to no good! I had so much fun in Texas. I had finally reached my first duty station. I was looking forward to being a regular soldier. There I was not in charge of anyone but myself. Whew!

Right away, I met a young lady who was also from South Carolina. Her name was Sergeant Inez Smith.

Smith and I had many things in common. We took road trips, spiced up for concerts, toured amusement parks and of course went to the clubs. Yes SAH! The two of us went on more adventures than anyone else I knew. We keep in touch still today. The best time we had was on a trip to New Orleans. You would not believe what happened in that city. What goes on in New Orleans, stays in New Orleans!

I was harassed by soldiers in Ft. Hood. Yep! I wasn't getting any quality brothers in Texas, so I started dating other races. The Caucasian males liked me a lot there. I met one that was very sweet to me. He would do anything for me. Guys called me names and harassed me because of who I chose to date. It was okay for them to date outside their race but not us black women. Due to the harassment, I asked for orders to be sent to another duty station.

Camp Stanley

Oh no! A fifteen-hour flight! Are you freaking kidding me? For a flight that long I had to have a few cocktails on the plane. Lol!

I was headed to South Korea for a one-year tour. I had heard so many nice things about being stationed there. South Korea was known for being one of the greatest places to shop. There it was like one huge shopping mall.

During this time, I was in the best shape ever. There we ran full speed up and down hills daily, no exceptions! Although I worked hard and did a lot of physical training, I had a great time in Korea.

I was stationed at Camp Stanley. This was a small base, and we all got along well. Huh? Well, some of us got along well, I guess I should say.

I quickly realized all good things come to an end. I began to get harassed by a few chicks that worked in the Mess Hall. They would do the catcalls and ask me out. I would say, "No". I did not find it flattering at all. Sadly, it was the only Mess Hall on the base, and I had to eat. I never responded angrily. I just kept it moving with hopes that they'd stop.

Finally, I was ready to date and get to know someone. I started dealing with a young lad. I called him, *"Tenderoni."* I was looking to try something different. I went to his barracks. I did not know that it wasn't good to sip on cocktails that someone else mixed.

That night I learned a great lesson. We were drinking, playing music with candles lit. The mood was set for something more than drinking. After having a few cocktails, we began to fool around. He asked if I had ever been blindfolded before.

Silly me, I let him blindfold me. This was a different experience for me indeed. One thing led to another and the music continued to play, and I remained blindfolded.

At the end of the moments, I removed the bandanna from my eyes. There they stood, the silly acting *chicks* from the Mess Hall. The young lad set me up! He knew the *butches* were hiding in the closet waiting to rape me. They were laughing and taunting me! I cussed and fussed but, they just laughed saying how they got me!

I ran up the hill to report the incident to the MPs (Military Police). In tears, I explained in detail what happened. I was told there was nothing that they could do. What just happened here? The Military Police said that I should not have been there. I was accused of being drunk and wearing small clothing.

I reported the incident to my chain of command as well. They said, "Report it to the MPs.". I was devastated, confused, and alone. I wanted to kill those people. How was I going to show my face in the Mess Hall again? I was never comfortable in the Mess Hall or on that base. I would pray every day for those hoes to die. Or that my tour would end soon.

Camp Jackson

Yes! Yes! My number had been called. I was chosen to attend the Primary Leadership Development Course (PLDC). I was thrilled. That was the next step to becoming a sergeant.

I was also relieved that I did not have to see the *butches* or *young lad* for a few weeks. I thought that I could finally breathe and have peace.

Nope! I was chosen to be a student First Sergeant on the first day of training.

This was a huge step up from the platoon guide. The drill sergeants picked me because I looked innocent, so they thought. I felt picked on because I was young and the only female in charge. I had to oversee every student there. Imagine all the responsibility that came with this title. I appeared excited, but I was nervous. Those male students did not appreciate a young female overseeing them. Of course, I was given a hard time once again. As time passed, the assault began. I could not go to chow without being teased about my walk, smile, legs, or something.

I could not go to the latrine at night without someone touching me. One night, a drill sergeant felt me up. I was so nervous I almost peed on myself. He rubbed my behind, kissed my neck, and massage my vagina. I was going through this and had to be silent. I kept my mouth shut and tried to stay focused on passing the course. Like before, "Suck it up and move on soldier!"

North Carolina

Free at last! I was headed back to the states. Oh boy! I was now stationed in Ft. Bragg. I was working in a motor pool, driving trucks, and working hard while wearing a beret. I was hanging out and doing my thing there.

Here we go again, same old stuff again! One day my squad leader came up to my room with a delivery. He questioned me about where I was going. He gave me a compliment on my outfit, but that was not enough. He started touching me and the assault took place. He kept saying, "You know you like it."

I went to my company commander and reported the incident. Basically, it was swept under the rug. My squad leader was well accomplished and was up for a promotion. I felt like people were mistreating me. I knew that it was because I did the report. Things had gotten so bad for me there in Bragg.

One day, while gaging my pod, I fell from the top of my five-ton truck. My tailgate was not secured. I hit my head on the pavement and was knocked unconscious.

When the workers found me, no one called the paramedics. The platoon leader made me go to the field that evening. It was not until I had an episode of migraines that I was taken to the TMC (Troop Medical Center) to be examined. I had been having migraines since the fall.

Finally, I was given an ultimatum. I had become so frustrated with the way I was being treated. I continued to file reports and complained about soldiers. For my silence, the commander granted me a stateside swap.

Georgia

I was then relocated to Ft. Stewart. There, I was faced with another dilemma. I just could not get a freaking break! I finally realized; it was not easy being me! However, I knew someone had to be. I had made the cutoff score and was owed back pay. I told my chain of command and no one seemed to care.

So, I filed a Congressional against the United States Army. What else was a soldier to do? I was fed up with the chain of command giving me their behinds to kiss.

It was time for me to defend myself.

Using diplomacy got me nowhere! The chain of command was furious with my choice of actions, but they had to respect them. They were too busy to assist me. "The drill sergeants didn't care about me!" I was later promoted to Sergeant and was given all my back money. What a journey!

CHAPTER SIX
Here is the Thing

What is love?

Does anyone really know the true meaning? People often say, "Love is blind". Wow no! People are blind. Not seeing what is really in front of them. So many of us are in crazy relationships. We all marry for various reasons.

Have you ever loved someone? I mean loved them enough to marry. Has someone ever made you feel that they loved you back? They treated you so kindly and gave you much love. They would whisper in your ear the sweetest things. Can you remember being treated to the finest wines and dining? Remember how they were always on your side no matter what?

I was off the chain before I got married. I was a party animal and I was in a motorcycle club. I had a ball! I was not bothering anyone and dared anyone to bother me. After marriage, I had to change. I eased up with the drinking because my mate did not drink. I resigned from the motorcycle club and parties. I was happily married.

Once my cousin, Brandon Gregory (BG) said, "I bet all the salt and pepper shakers in all the grocery stores that you and Randy are together." That was cute and funny, but true. Randy Bobbit and

I were inseparable. We were like Bonnie and Clyde, Sonny and Cher, Mork and Mindy. People would never see one of us without the other.

Eventually, I learned he was putting up a front! Suddenly, there was chaos. Randy flipped on me. Little did I know, Randy was Dr. Jekyll and Mr. Hyde. His hidden red flags had been exposed. I was blindsided by his behavior. He began to curse, argue, and threaten me. I wondered what happened to him. I tried to seek help, but he did not want assistance.

None of my friends believed me when I told them of his drastic change. Especially, my friend, Tam Laney. She thought he was the sweetest guy in the world. On the other hand, my friend Renee Dawson felt he was a suspect and my homeboy, Kevin Studer felt bad about it too.

Kevin came over one night with a twelve-pack of Coors Light apologizing. He said he was wrong about Randy, "Please forgive me?" I saw him in the streets looking bad!" Up until this day he shakes his head whenever he thinks about it.

Others would speak of the kind, giving, caring Randy. He would cut people's grass, cut guys' hair, try holding Bible study, and always had kind words for others. He would wake me up to read the Word.

After three months of being mistreated, I turned into someone that I did not recognize in the mirror. I was trying to sleep one night when I heard yelling in the living room. I got up to see what was going on. It was Randy sitting on the sofa screaming for no reason. "EH! EH! EH! EH!" I asked him to stop yelling but, he got louder. It was like a demonic spirit had taken over his mind and body. "Please stop yelling," I said with anger. He turned to me with hatred and disgust and said, "I am not yelling." Facing the television, he yelled softly, "eh! eh! eh! eh!" I fell to my knees looking towards the ceiling. "Oh God! Why has thou forsaken me? Why me Lord!" I yelled.

My mother, Dawn Gilbert, said she would have left him then! I stupidly stayed. One day Randy came home yelling and screaming at the top of his lungs accusations. He had extreme turmoil on the membrane! I continued with my dinner and listened. I gave Randy the floor! I tried to keep my composure. I was trying to be pa**tient**.

Once he sat down, I stood up. I walked slowly behind him as he watched television. I grabbed him by his neck.

My small hands had a grip that was getting stronger and tighter. Before I knew it, I had taken his shirt and tighten it around his neck. He began gasping for air. Oh! That moment felt so good. My adrenaline was rushing, and I could not stop! I was given strength from somewhere. I threw him across the room! I had become so furious with the sound of his voice, his actions, disrespect, and deceit.

He started yelling and ran into the bathroom to look at his neck. "You're crazy!" he shouted! Randy ran outside fading into the darkness. I was relaxed, relieved, and rejuvenated. I was done with all the turmoil and ready to journey on. This dude had no idea what I wanted to do to him!

I remember people telling me not to leave. Why should I have stayed? Is it because they stayed in their unhappy marriages for years? One stayed because of their children. One did not want to feel like a failure. Several slept in separate rooms in hopes of change. No! Get out while you have the chance. No one should settle. I refused to allow anything or anyone to get in my way to destroy my happiness.

Here's the thing! Ten years had passed, and now he has decided to contact me. Randy apologized for it all. He assured me that it wasn't anything that I had done. At first, I was surprised to hear from him. I soon realized that he was sincere. I accepted his apology, and my life moved on as we know it. I do not hate the young lad.

We all make mistakes! I'll always feel that my ex cared nothing about me!

If you're in a relationship and you feel lonely or abandoned, leave. If you're wondering why me Lord, keep praying. If you're guessing that things will change, they won't. If you have that gut feeling you can do better, just do it. If you love yourself more, start packing. It doesn't matter how long you've been in a relationship; you should always choose happiness!

Step out on faith. God will give you your heart's desire. It's up to you what you choose to do with it.

CHAPTER SEVEN

Bumps in The Road

"Over the river and through the woods…" Just a little tune I'd sang as I traveled the roads. That is what helped to keep me sane! By this time in my life, I have experienced many life challenges and detours. I have had to endure the good, the bad, and the ugly. Many days I had to laugh to keep from crying. Despite it all, I still haven't slowed down. I kept it moving. Life is too precious to waste time on discouraging bumps in the road.

It was Holy Week. Good Friday to be exact. My friend, the City Slicker, and I were making plans for Easter. I was looking forward to the beach, the park or just a walk at Seaport Village. There was a lot going on in the village.

I thought the City Slicker and I were having fun together. At least that is what he led me to believe. We began texting Friday morning, a text here, one there, and then Wham! He began sending mean texts. I could not understand it. I was thinking it was a joke or maybe he texted the wrong person.

I decided to text him from my other cell phone. Sure, he began texting back. He thought that I was another woman and asked if I would send a picture. I did! I downloaded a picture from black hairstyles and sent it to him. "Oh okay! I remember you," he replied. "You're beautiful as always. I just can't remember your name," I responded, "My name is Toni, but my friends call me Tipp."

Wow! The City Slicker and Tipp texted one another for the rest of the day. He even texted while he was at work. That's something he never would have done for me. Cool beans!

When I text from my phone, he ignored my texts. That burnt me up. I thought to myself, "No problem man!" I kept right on being Tipp. It was time for Tipp and her friends to hit the Gaslamp. The downtown area where it all goes down. He wanted Tipp to swing by the club he managed first. Of course, that wasn't going to happen. I downloaded another picture. This time the female was wearing dress clothes in the photo. He was saying how much he wished he could join Tipp and her friends.

The night had come to an end and now Tipp was at home. *El Stupido* asked if he could visit her. Mind you, the two have never spoken on the phone and never met.

Tipp sent the City Slicker her address. At two o'clock a.m. he was headed to Tipp's house. Tipp texted him, "When you get to the complex, park outside the gate. Walk through the door beside the gate. Go down the sidewalk until you see the dumpsters. Make a right turn and go up the stairs until you get to the third floor." "What is your apartment number?" he asked. "I'm in apartment

T32," Tipp replied. He arrived to see he had been pranked! I laughed wondering how did he feel being played?

Got him! I had no idea what he said or did. I blocked him from both phones.

Picture this. It was the year 1999. That's when I met Boston. He was my first real and true love. After four years of dating, he decided to move. He had gotten frustrated with his job and wanted to do something different. My cousin, K. Michelle would always make jokes about him moving.

We were at the peak of our relationship where things were going well and stupid me decided to relocate as well. Somehow I didn't get the memo that I could not go. Well, that's what his mother implied. She told him that she didn't think I should go. Oh yes! His mom was the main reason we broke up. She let it be known that I didn't need to relocate to Massachusetts. I was crushed.

One day I stepped outside of my body. I saw myself lying there on the bed weeping as if someone had died. I was furious! After an hour, I picked myself up, washed my face, and put on something cute. That's the day I enrolled in the WU. I was already working two jobs full time and decided to do more. I kept myself busy.

Again! I came across another bump. His name was Fort Mill. Before getting involved, my sister Carmela Gilbert warned him. "Don't mess up young man," she said. She and my brother Connor Thomas were very protective. I loved that about them! Well, Ft. Mill didn't listen. He was extremely nice at first. He couldn't get enough of hanging with me. He called me Cali. I was kind to this gentleman. Little did I know, he was a true user! This guy did not know me at all. He was planning something serious. He thought I was going to move in with him. He wanted me to help him catch up on his bills and assist him with his family's land. No way!

He was mean to me because I had my own place. I ended up choking and punching him! I must admit, this bump blindsided me!

I ended up with a Hispanic man named Mr. Padilla this time. I was trying something new. He was a few years older than I. I must admit, we had the most fun together. Trips to Mexico and all. I enjoyed hanging out with him. One Thanksgiving our plans were doomed. He called crying telling me his mother passed. From that moment on, I was committed to listening to his problems. My group at church put him on the prayer list. We continued to see each other. Eight months out and the shenanigans began.

I was leaving my VA appointment and noticed him in the parking lot. I skipped over to the truck excited to see him. But it wasn't him. It was a woman instead. I learned that he had a girlfriend and his mother was not dead! Not only was he lying about being single, but he also killed his mom!

I'll never forget Tony from York. He was a compulsive liar. He bought me a ring and a lot of other things. He had me hanging out at *"his house"*. I later discovered the house really belonged to his grandmother. A broad at a bike party told me he was also married. I was deeply crushed! I gathered my bat, my knife, and riding partners and headed to York.

I drove while Renee Dawson and Brandon Gregory were naked in the back seat. I played Fantasia's 'When I See You' about ten times the way there and back. When I finally arrived, I put a hurting on Tony. He will think twice about playing games with another woman.

I became so tired of men and their shenanigans. As if they don't have any compassion, respect, nor love for anyone. How dare they lead someone on! How dare they use women like me! I was tired of the lies! I took a hiatus from relationships. That was the best decision ever!

I didn't care about anything or nobody. I began focusing on myself exclusively. Some people aren't strong enough to deal with life's deviations. But I am grateful for the strength and peace of mind that Jesus gave me.

Although I ran into many drawbacks, I continued my life's journey. I refused to let anything, or anyone destroy my mind or my heart. I was determined to love and be loved.

"BRETHREN, I COUNT NOT MYSELF TO HAVE APPREHENDED: BUT THIS ONE THING I DO, FORGETTING THOSE THINGS WHICH ARE BEHIND, AND REACHING FORTH UNTO THOSE THINGS WHICH ARE BEFORE, I PRESS TOWARD THE MARK FOR THE PRIZE OF THE HIGH CALLING OF GOD IN CHRIST JESUS." PHILIPPIANS 3:13-14.

Bump!!

Oh, what a time I had at my cousin's Cassy's wedding. It was everything that I imagined it would be. I did what was expected of me!. Of course, I was a bridesmaid. Cassy made sure that everyone in the family played an important role in her wedding. We made it *do what it does!* I didn't meet many eligible bachelors though.

Afterward, I headed to my mom's house to change into something more comfortable. It was time for the family to get *buck wild*. That would consist of drinking, dancing, eating, laughing, cursing, name-calling, smoking, and lounging.

Out of nowhere, a tall, dark, handsome, and shiny stallion with sparkling white teeth approached me. Apparently, he had been asking people about me during the ceremony.

His name was Kelsey Gilmore. His friends called him K.G.

"Wow! I am pleased to meet you." I replied. One conversation led to another. We danced and chatted all throughout the long day. We had a few drinks and talked about family, friends, and our lives. I remembered him singing in the choirs during revivals in the past. Lol!

We started talking on the phone from that day on. We began to spend a lot of time together.

It was his idea to take a lovely trip to Maryland. Our friendship grew great quickly and we enjoyed each other. People were happy to see us together. He and I became close friends. I finally was with a kindhearted man that I trusted. Not all men made me feel safe like he did. I was finally able to let my guards down.

My friends teased me often about how this black stallion chased me all around the wedding and how I played hard to get. "He would not stop until he got you." They constantly reminded me. I fell for the *Okie Doke*! I felt like I made a decent decision and I was happy to be in the relationship. Our relationship was free from drama.

What was I thinking? After one trip, he called me cursing and yelling. He wouldn't let me say one word. I could not believe the things that I was hearing. This man *flipped* on me right before Thanksgiving. Did he forget who he was talking too? Did he realize what he was saying? Was he on drugs? Then, the ugly prune hung up on me! I was mad! Carmela was furious! All the ladies talked about what they were going to do whenever they saw that black snake. I was afraid of what one of us would do. Family sticks together when bad things happen. Especially, the women. I'd hear them say:

"I saw my cousin Dharma on New Year's." She yelled,

"Amada! Amanda!"

"Did you hear the news about K.G?"

"Carmela saw Kelsey at a party around Christmas."

"She tasered him right in his chest."

"He was shaking and trembling! HAHA! She did what she did with a straight face!"

I yelled, "Roll out the red carpet!"

"Champagne for everyone! I did a dance to the good news. "Some guys play way too much! They should be honest with women, no matter what."

YOU SHALL REAP WHAT YOU SOW GALATIANS 6:7-10

CHAPTER EIGHT
The Finest City

"Hey! What's up Cousin? What's going on in the Carolinas? You need to be on the Westside!" That was the call I received from my cousin Ceno Thomas. He and his wife Dharma Thomas invited me to San Diego. Yes! San Diego, the *Finest City*.

At that moment, my mind started racing. I paced the floor in eagerness. I researched the place where my fresh start would begin.

I was used to starting over because of my years in the military. My cousins had given me something to look forward to. By this time, I had divorced, and I needed a change of scenery.

I made up my mind. "California, here I come!" I gave away and sold all my possessions. I packed everything I could fit into my Mustang and drove to California. Just like that. Nothing nor anyone was holding me in the Carolinas. I stepped out on faith and left with a new life in mind.

I learned why San Diego was called the Finest City. The city is something to see. It is known for its beautiful beaches, parks, art galleries, museums, and gardens.

It's a lovely day at Balboa Park, the renowned San Diego Zoo and artist studios. I can't forget its warm weather and the food, Oh My Gosh!

Although I've always believed, San Diego was for lovers, I had a great time living there I dreamed it to be a land of opportunity. Ceno suggested I go there and allow the Veterans Affairs to assist me with whatever I needed. It had been years since I departed the Army and I didn't have all my benefits. He knew of my chances in San Diego. The VA facilities there are great. I would get appointments so quickly. My primary care doctor put me in the best physical therapy, occupational therapy, acupuncture, and dental care available. I met a lot of kind people there.

My crew consisted of Katie Steele, Donna Simms, Mrs. Octavia, Marie Glover, Tina Jacobs, and sister Shelia Houston. I can't forget 'the three musketeers'. That consisted of me, Dottie Greene and the Duke of Earle. I had a great time with those ladies. I am grateful for them. Oh, my goodness! The three of us had the most amazing time as we helped serve the community.

I had a great time with those ladies. They kept me on my toes. We would meet for coffee, conversation, lunch, dinner, cocktails, advice, movies or fellowship, or for me to seek advice.

I'll never forget karaoke on Thursday, and Sunday It was funny because out of the group, only one of us would sing. We would go there to support Donna. I assisted patients with rides to their doctor appointments. Once a month, I served the homeless at Father Joe's Village.

I joined the Common Ground Theatre. Their mission was to produce classics and new works by and about people of African descent that entertained, educated, and connected with audiences of all ages, cultures, and backgrounds. This theater was the only African American Theater in San Diego.

With Common Ground, I was one of the casts, occasional stage managers and I was also a member of the board of directors. I was honored to have worked with Mrs. Francine Dewitt and Marie Franklin.

I was also a member of the Martin Luther King Jr. Community Choir, with a fabulous director Ken Anderson. The Martin Luther King Jr choir was an all-volunteer, non-profit organization with one primary purpose. That was to sing Gospel, Negro Spirituals, hymns, and engaging wholeheartedly in Performing Arts. We raised funds for educational grants for San Diego County high school seniors pursuing a college degree in Visual or Performing Arts.

I enjoyed being a member of the Dennis T. Williams, Post 310 American Legion. I met some wonderful people while attending. Man, oh man, I've had my share of fun there.

There were a few kind people at the church I attended. One mastermind was Mrs. Alvina Rushmore. She's how I got started helping the homeless downtown. She was like the humanitarian of San Diego. Mrs. Rushmore would help and love on anyone in need. I am glad that I had the chance to meet her. I met a group that gave me tickets to be on the television game show, *Let's Make a Deal*.

It was like being at a party. Also, a cool couple, Carlos and Monerey McVay gave me tickets to the Bishop T.D. Jakes show. Both experiences were very exciting and interesting.

Believe me, all things weren't great living in the *Finest City*. I had a setback when I arrived. My living conditions weren't like I was used to. I moved from a luxury loft in the Carolinas into a Pit.

Ha! I didn't start out in the pit.

I landed there.

The Pit

This place was like no other place that I have ever lived. It was tiny, cold, dreadful, and lonely, but clean. I bet it was the cleanest on the block. I refused to live in filth whether the place is up to par or not. The owner refused to get the stove to work. I had to cook on hot plates, use the microwave, or eat out.

I bought a small refrigerator for my food.

The bathroom had no walls and only a frame and floor. That's it! Living there was just like living in a tent in the field. It was a clean tent with a TV, and a refrigerator with green and white decor. It was extremely cold because the owner never put in installation. I was delirious from the cold. My long johns, blankets, quilts, scarfs, and toboggans weren't enough. I had to sleep with one eye open. One was to get some rest and the other to stand guard from the ants that were marching on the ceiling. I couldn't kill them all and I just wanted to sleep.

I could just hear them singing:
"The biscuits in the Army
The biscuits in the Army
They say they mighty fine
One rolled off the table
And killed a friend of mine"

I didn't know if I was tired, cold, or crazy. I was out of my mind in that pit. However, I was determined and would not let that stop me. I'd take a walk at least three days a week. Walking was my way of meditation. It cleared my mind, helped me get ideas, and lose weight. I was in a fight against Veterans Affairs. My purpose for the relocation was to obtain and earn my V.A. benefits. Yet, I was surviving, I cried every day in the pit.

I would sing an old negro spiritual:
"Nobody knows the trouble I've seen

Nobody knows my sorrow"

I think I understood Mr. Louis Armstrong.

I continued to attend church every Sunday, donate to most organizations, and helped the homeless.

Two good friends came to visit me from Carolina. They were K. Love and Renee Dawson. I remember feeling embarrassed when they arrived. They couldn't believe my living arrangements. I'm certain they talked about me when they returned home.

While in town, I showed them a good time. My cousin, Ceno invited us to a fabulous party in the Gaslamp. It was extremely nice. There was bottle service all night. Renee would holler, "Cee let me get that!" We got drunk!

K. Love drove us back to the DoubleTree where they had a room. First, we stopped by Subway to buy some bread and get some salt. Finally, I was relieved from the pit for a few days. But, it had become my home for months.

My time spent in this awful pit would do one or two things. One, make me angry. The thought of me possibly making the biggest mistake of my life. Or two, looking at things differently and taking it as a learning experience. Sometimes we must make sacrifices to get what we need or want. Being so low in the pit, I realized that my only way was up.

I wasn't successful when it came to relationships either. The guys I met just could not cut it with me. Living in Paradise, as it's called and still no luck! My friends would always joke and say, "You needed to go to the Carolinas to bring a man back." With this thought in mind, I didn't give up on the men. I am glad that I did not. I ended up meeting a *tenderoni,* however. He was a young man named Mustapha also known as the Chosen One. He was quite the gentleman. With him, I realized that *chivalry* was not dead. I am grateful for the times we spent together.

I learned so much about people, life and myself being around him.

The City's Finest?

I was in a horrible car accident, October 6, 2018. I totaled my beautiful convertible Mustang. Patience was her name. The other car involved in the accident involved a blue compass jeep. Meanwhile, the supposedly, city finest (National City Police Department) came up to my car yelling. "Do you know what just happened here? Do you know what you've done?" I started explaining what happened and he walked away. A chubby, white, sandy brown-haired cop looking like Spanky of the Little Rascals and reminded me of a drill sergeant.

The hood of Patience was straight in the air. I couldn't see anything in front of me. I smelled fumes of some sort and my face was burning, guessing from my airbags. The cop wouldn't let me out of the car. I was terrified and alone. I didn't know if I was going to be shot, killed, or beaten as which was commonly read and seen on the news. Another black person killed by the police for no reason. I was totally nervous and uncomfortable.

The police walked to the front of the car, then back to me fussing. He finally came and asked me for my license, registration, and insurance information. I asked if it was ok to reach to the floor without being shot because my purse had fallen during the accident. He yelled, "Yes!".

He accused me of hitting his car. I knew this cop was lying. I hit a blue Jeep. Cops drive black explorers in National City.

I felt harassment approaching. By this time, my nerves were destroyed. I began to panic and freaked out!

He finally allowed me to get out of the vehicle. My entire front end was smashed in. I could barely walk. The paramedics and fire department were never called. The cops never asked if I was injured or if I was ok. He just yelled.

Along comes another cop. I was trying to explain how I felt harassed. He kept asked why.

I responded, "This guy accused me of smelling like alcohol. Why would he do that? Now I am nervous and concerned. He didn't give me the breath test, just a few arm movements." Then Spanky returned my credentials. Still, my car was totaled, and no paramedics were called. I had to walk home from the scene of the crime.

Not once did any cop offer me a ride or call the paramedics.

As I was walking home, I passed the young lady in the blue compass Jeep. She asked, "Why is no one talking to me? What was taking so long?" I replied, "They were too busy harassing me!" When Spanky noticed me talking to her, he rushed down to where we were standing and placed his hands on his hips. I limped on down the street toward home. I cried the whole way home.

I had a terrible panic attack that night. I could not believe that National City Police would treat someone that way. I did seek medical attention on my own. I learned that I had sprained my neck, my back, and reinjured my leg.

I will never forget, nor would I allow my comrades to forget that the National City Police harassed me, a female. A citizen who served the country, a disabled veteran, who got no respect from the National City Police department. I do not trust the police today because of that incident and what I saw on the news regarding Police brutality. I and the entire world are uncomfortable with police. I don't know how to react whenever they are around. I pray that I am never in need of assistance. I don't know who I'd call because they have proven to be incompetent in serving.

I've given the *Finest City* nine years of my life. I had been thinking about doing something different now. Maybe I should relocate or maybe start something new. Well, the jury was still out on that at that time! I was thinking about it.

Lord
I'm Stepping Out
From my
Comfort Zone......
Letting go of me,
Holding on to you!

CHAPTER NINE
The Agony of the Sanctuary

There are many different types of hurt. Some suffer mentally, physically, emotionally, and even spiritually. What do you think of when you hear the word *church*? A building used for Christian religious activities or worship services. A place people go to learn and understand the Gospel. A sanctuary filled with people who love Jesus. A place of refuge and safety. People attend for one reason or another.

The sanctuary has always been my *Safe Haven*. This is where I would run to every Sunday to escape the dangers of the world, to clear my mind, to praise, worship, sing, dance, shout, and feel free from it all. This is where I would meet Jesus.

"For where two or three are gathered together in my name, there am I in the midst of them."
Matthew 18:20 (KJV)

Of course, I am not perfect, and I had never pretended to be. I was a little something different. (Laugh out loud) I know that

I did wrong and that's why I ran to the sanctuary on Sunday.

Come one, come all and come as you are. I go as I am, weary, wounded, and sad. My week seems to always go better once I attend. I don't feel the pain from my injuries as much. I'm not as weak. The church was my fellowship place. I enjoyed going and receiving the Word of God, singing, worshipping, and being amongst Spirit-filled souls. I am grateful that my mom and grandmother got me involved at a young age. I prayed that I'd continue to grow in Jesus Christ.

Church has changed a lot. Before the people were able to praise, worship, and testify freely. It's not like that anymore. Nowadays, everything done in the church is being shared on social media.

Some people don't want to share their testimony on social media because people dare to share your business on their personal social media pages. No place is private anymore.

There was one church in California that I enjoyed. The pastor there was one of a kind. The mission statement was one of the things that grabbed my attention. "Striving to give hurting people new hope, a new life, and a new way." That is something that I have been doing for years. Reaching out to others and blessing them in any way possible.

This Master Pastor, his nickname to many, talked about the "Core Value."

Many of the people there only cared about the value of a dollar. All folks want to know is how to get over on someone. They would use their sickness, grandchildren, or age to finagle money. They would use sceneries like, "I lost my job. Can the church help me out?" or "My car is down, and I need medications. Pastor, can the church help me?" It was always something!

The Pastor would also talk about the past. He said, "We are all an EX something!" He'd say, "Stop putting on scuba gear, diving in, pulling up folks past." Whoo! That's a good one! That was the L in Core Value. Leave the past behind.

Did some of the church members hear the Pastor? Nope! There was a time when the church members used someone's past to stop them from becoming Pastor. Let the past go, people! Let it go!

There were a lot of bad people however, not all of them. I have grown to love several of them. I have good friendships with most of them.

Something Terrible Happened to Me

Picture this, a warm beautiful day in August. I was in one of the best moods ever. I was excited to hang out with my good friend Marie Glover. I bought in advance VIP tickets to a concert on El Cajon Blvd. I pull up to the concert, looking quite lovely, I would say.

I was told that I could arrive early and mingle with people before the show. I did just that! When I arrived, I spoke with people walking to the building and to others who were standing outside. I went to the doors and they were locked! "What in the world was going on?" is what thought. Through the glass doors, I saw people walking around on the inside, sitting at the tables and in the chairs behind the VIP section.

No one would let me in. Several women from the church were sitting at a table near the doors. They just looked at me. Not one of them said a word. Then one lady, Mrs. Evil Knievel, started yelling, "The door is locked! The door is locked!" "Wow, really Sherlock?" I couldn't believe everyone, except me, was able to get in. Evil Knievel did this same thing to me and others at church. I really wasn't surprised!

Along came a chic I had never seen before. I didn't get her name, but she had bluish hair. She asked me to come back later because she couldn't let me in. At first, I thought about saying something to her. Then I realized she had nothing to do with it. I knew that she didn't know me.

Angry, pissed, and furious I hurried to my car, I hurried to my car! I had to call someone and tell them about what had happened. I could not calm down. My heart was beating fast and I was breathing heavily. My cousin Dharma told me to catch my breath and get my composure.

"Don't let them still your Joy Cousin," she said. I called my friend whom I was meeting. She couldn't understand what happened. She stated that she was on her way. I was so mad. My peers called me Mad Maxx! I wanted to leave but those tickets were fifty dollars. Hell No, I stayed!

I received a call from inside the concert from another friend, Mrs. Jasmine Garrett. She wanted to know where I was because my name was on her table. I explained to her what happened. I told her I was watching from my car and I saw her, and the others go into the building.

Finally, Marie arrived, and we went to the building. The ladies at the table looked at me sideways. An usher came and walked us to our table. It was the last table of the section. Why wasn't I surprised?

Little girl Blue came up to me apologizing. She said the ladies didn't like me. "They told me to let everyone in the building before you but, you left." She repeated, "When you came to the door, the other ladies said, "Do not let her in."

[31] What, then, shall we say in response to these things? If God is for us, who can be against us.

Romans 8:31-39 (NIV)

I accepted her apology and sat down with my friends. I had gotten so upset my head began to hurt. I mean, a migraine from the gates of Wow. Then my neck started tensing up. The pain went through my whole body down to my toes. All I could think of was the women who wouldn't let me in.

I struggled the whole night to sit amongst my enemies. There's no excuse for Christians to act that way. I wasn't sure how to act around some of them. I was quite skeptical about my return to church after that.

People often say, "All churches are alike. This is not true. I found a place where the people have a heart of gold. Whenever I walked through the doors, I felt loved. The Pastor was so smart, kept it real, and was loving. I enjoyed listening to old familiar Hymns at my old church. At this new church, I was much happier. I told everyone about my new church. My bike club members, college friends, soldiers, and my friends I met along the way. The Wilson was a true Safe Haven, and no one was ever turned away. Whenever I go back there it feels like I had never left. This church overflowed with peace, love, and the family feel. There's no place like home I can truly say.

CHAPTER TEN
The Missing Piece

Oh My! He gently pressed me against the wall. He kissed my lips as he rubbed his fingers through my thick natural hair. He massaged my breasts as he sucked on my ear lobes, then my neck. "Oh, babe you feel so good," I said. Then he spread my legs as he lifted my gown and pushed my thong aside. He entered me with his smooth Mandingo. I enjoyed the slow long thrusts until I woke up. Ha! Ha! Ha! I can dream of this man all day, every day!

I once heard that friends were the best lovers. In my case, it's true. One of my closest friends asked me a question once. "Do you want to be married or happy?" I wanted to be happily married.

I know it's weird, but I had always imagined that we'd end up together. Farfetched for some minds, but not impossible.

I'm a believer in astrology and zodiac signs I've was told by my Vietnamese friend, Ms. Lihn, that there is a lot of truth to zodiac signs. I am a Taurus and my closest friend was a Cancer. He had a smooth butterscotch complexion, nice smile, bald, tall, and good looking. He was quiet and very patient. Marc Ellis and I have been friends for over twenty years. It didn't matter what was going on in our lives, we had each other's back. He's a smooth operator. He would remain calm through the toughest situations. Unlike me! I am like a *grenade*! I am lovely on the outside with a passion for green, but do not twist nor pull me, because I will explode on you. Marc, he'd think before he reacted. He usually didn't get upset nor fussed as I would've.

Talk about my match! He had a mouth like mine. People often said that I had a smart mouth. However, I see myself more as a comedian. I called Marc, "Smarty-pants." Yes! He had a sense of humor too. Wow! I loved it! This guy was something. He made me laugh and that is something very hard to do. I thank him for the laughs.

Marc has always been able to get me to simmer down. He knew how to keep things simple. Unlike myself, I was more like a torpedo. He had a sweet spirit, warm heart, and was very calming. We are alike in many ways, but different also. Our opposites attracted us to one another.

Now, don't let Marc fool you. Although he was understanding, he didn't play. He is the type that would not walk anyone to walk over him. He knew how to keep me in line. That kind of stuff turns me on! I loved him being on my team. He knew how to keep his composure.

He was my confidant, friend, pen pal, and a familiar piece. His compassion and gentleness kept us in sync. Every time we would see each other, our eyes would meet, and he'd strike my heart. I'm sure he felt it too. I haven't felt this type of deep connection for a long time. When he called my name, his voice sent chills through my bones and body. Now the phrase, "You're everything I never knew I always wanted." made sense.

Marc called me the missing piece to his puzzle. "Whenever I was gone, a piece of my heart missed you." he'd say. We were made for each other, no matter who we were with.

No mountains were too high, no rivers too deep, nor valleys too wide, that could keep us apart. We continued to stay in touch over the years.

This kind of soul was also a gentleman. He'd open and close doors for me. His presence stunned me. On our very first official date, he joked about it. It was something that he wanted to do. *Believe me you*, I was happy yet, I wondered.

You know how you have those handsome, cool, and charming guys who say what they feel. Yes exactly! He was too cool for gentle stuff. I guess when someone cares about you, there's no limit to what he will do for you. He could cook too! The way to my heart is cooking.

I love a man that cooks and can put it down in the bedroom. He would cook whatever I wanted to eat whenever I requested him to. Not too much grease, spices, or anything. What he cooked for me was always just right.

He was my very own personal chef. He had strong, smooth hands that massaged my shoulders, hips, and feet whenever needed.

The first guy ever! That's a shame! The guys in my past had been so freaking selfish, but not Marc. He cared about my feelings. That meant a lot to me. That's why I would do anything for him.

My cousin Dexter Woody would joke about Marc and me being soulmates. Platonic partners, with a lifelong bond, two into one, Ying and yang! Woody thought the two of us we're cute together.

I loved my best friend and yes we were cute together. I prayed that we remained close for a lifetime. Some people search their whole lives and never find friendship as special as ours was. I thank God for my dear friend Marc Ellis.

He is also a great Dad! Now, this is the one thing that truly amazed me about him. He'll do any and everything for his children and grandchildren. The way his face brightened whenever he spoke of them. He often showed pictures of them. Oh my, he is such a happy Dad. I was so proud of him for that.

Although Marc has a lot of good qualities for a man, he was far from being perfect. Of course, no one is perfect. He had his flaws and made mistakes. Only God can judge him. I thank him for never throwing my past in my face. We made vows to live for the moment and love each other no matter what. I thank him for loving me the way I am and for never judging me.

> **"Do not judge, or you too will be judged. [2] For in the same way you judge others, you will be judged, and with the measure you use, it will be measured to you.**
>
> **Matthew 7:1,2 (NIV)**

All things are be made beautiful with God. My heart will forever be with Marc! I pray that we'll always remain friends. Our friendship inspired me to write poetry.

I also prayed that he got what he been searching for. I know that he wasn't happy in his current situation. He had a mean, conniving and backstabbing mate. What goes around, comes around! Good luck Marc Ellis!

MATTHEW 5:16

Inserted private inside joke to some readers!

"Hide your friend, hide your uncle and hide your cousin." Laugh out loud! Only a few people would get that joke.

POETRY
At Last!

We greet each other

Our lips will touch

Oh, how I love you so much

Your tender love

Your warm embrace

Finally, we're faced to face

In your arms

I'm held so tight

God! This feels so right.

We're both excited

Our hearts beat fast

We are so happy

Together at last!

First Sight!

I believe in love at first sight
I met a kind fella one gentle night
We laughed, smiled, joked but didn't touch
To cross the line, would be too much
We chat a while to figure out
To learn what each other was all about
We enjoyed the moments as much as we could
We drew a line where we both stood
I told him that I was moving away
He asked if he could make me stay
I left Carolina to return again
Back in the arms of my Dearest Friend
I don't remember the exact date
I knew in my heart it was only fate
I wasn't sure what to make of this all
I waited patiently for his call.
I know our friendship is very true
For him there's nothing I won't do.
Your love I'll hold unto so tight
With you, my life it feels so right.

The Last Time

I was gone for so long

I didn't miss his touch

He begged and plead that he miss me so much.

I once was his token

That he placed on the shelf

My heart was so broken

He blamed himself.

The damage was done

I was on my way

Take care my friend was all I could say

This is the last time

I couldn't take any more

I followed my mind

And walked out of the door!

Broken

The
Crashing
The
Burns.
The
Lost's
The
Earns.
The
Hopes
The
Dreams.
The
Pain
The
Stings.
Do you have a band aid?
For a broken heart,
It will not heal,
But it's a good start.

Once Loved

Light turned into darkness

Sunlight into rain

The one that I loved

Has caused me pain.

He once said

I was the love of his Life.

Now I am feeling torture

From lies, deceit and strife.

I don't know what to do

I am so torn apart.

He didn't realize

He'd break my heart.

I was once loved.

CHAPTER ELEVEN
Good Grief!

"Now Amanda, how are you feeling? You were finally able to get some stuff off your chest." "PLEASE SIT-DOWN MRS. BOBBIT!" Stop swinging your arms in the air ma'am, Dr. Stephens shouted!

Good Grief! "I am as happy as a camel on Wednesday!" I said. After all the treatment for anxiety, TBI, MST and PTSD, I am feeling good! I have got to be. At least that is what I tell myself. I must think positive no matter what.

I can truly say, "God is Amazing." He has blessed me tremendously with good health and strength. He has helped me through many obstacles. I have always kept my faith no matter what happened.

"I am proud of you Amanda," Dr. Stephens stated. What are you doing for entertainment? Do you have a support group? Are you more in touch with your family than before? How was your trip? Do you plan to start a family? Why do people call you the Choker? Can you respond? Keep sending out the *Wowo Sunshine* messages. You are making more of a difference than you know. We have six minutes left. Remember this is our last session. You are my last patient here at this VA facility. Dr. Stephens had a lot of questions and comments. Wow!

My response:
> "I first want to thank you. I have been seeing you for eight years. Not sure that I would like to meet anyone else. HA! HA! HA! I don't have time to answer your questions. It's not easy being me, but someone must be! "Life is good for me and I can't help but smile. I sing because I'm happy I sing because I'm free. I live my life to the fullest. It's not easy being me!"

I had a long debate with the voices in my head. The debate was whether to tell this story or not. As you have read, THE VOICES WON! My story.

> "And the day came when the risk to remain tight in a bud was more painful than the risk it took to blossom"
>
> ~Anais Nin

Final Note:

    Amanda has lived a devastating, frightening, interesting, and quite unique life. There was the feeling of having no one to turn to for a long time and she was too afraid to sleep. Amanda's only way of peace was her walk-in faith. God's grace and mercy has really helped her through. She still resides in California where she enjoys the beautiful beaches, the sunny days, walks in the park and continues to donate her time to help others. Although it's not easy being Amanda, she knows someone must be!

www.ingramcontent.com/pod-product-compliance
Lightning Source LLC
Chambersburg PA
CBHW071413290426
44108CB00014B/1802